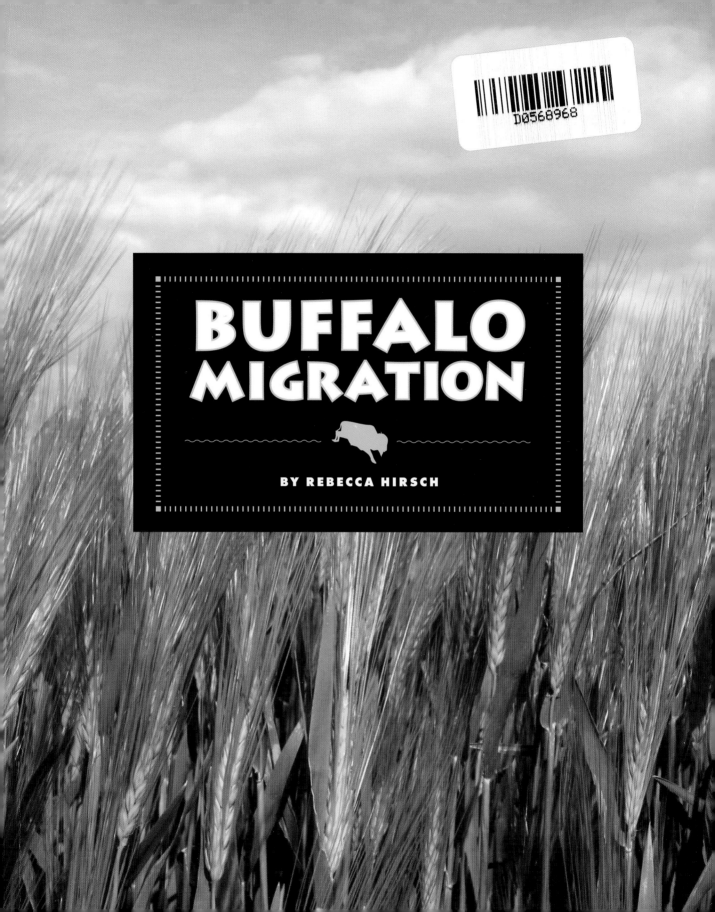

BUFFALO MIGRATION

BY REBECCA HIRSCH

The Child's World®

Published by The Child's World®
1980 Lookout Drive • Mankato, MN 56003-1705
800-599-READ • www.childsworld.com

ACKNOWLEDGMENTS
The Child's World®: Mary Berendes, Publishing Director
Content Consultant: Dr. Tanya Dewey,
    University of Michigan Museum of Zoology
The Design Lab: Design and production
Red Line Editorial: Editorial direction

PHOTO CREDITS
Sebastien Burel/Dreamstime, cover (bottom), 2-3; Uko Jesita/Dreamstime,
cover (top), 1, back cover; Samuel Strickler/Dreamstime, 4-5; XNR
Productions, 7; Sascha Burkard/Dreamstime, 8, 27; Sharron Schiefelbein/
Dreamstime, 10-11; Stefan Ekernas/Dreamstime, 12; Vanessa Gifford/
Dreamstime, 13; Mighty Sequoia Studio/Shutterstock Images, 14; Kelly
Boreson/Dreamstime, 16-17; Sam Strickler/Shutterstock Images, 18-19;
Linda Bair/Dreamstime, 20-21; Scott Payne/Dreamstime, 22-23; Rinus
Baak/Dreamstime, 24; James Mattil/Dreamstime, 25; Arturo Limon/
Dreamstime, 28

Design elements: Uko Jesita/Dreamstime

ISBN 9781609736170
LCCN 2011940060

Printed in the United States of America

ABOUT THE AUTHOR: Rebecca Hirsch, PhD, is the author of several nonfiction books for children. A former biologist, she writes for children and young adults about science and the natural world. She lives with her husband and three daughters in State College, Pennsylvania.

TABLE OF CONTENTS

AMERICAN BUFFALO...4

MIGRATION MAP...6

KINGS OF THE PRAIRIE...8

HISTORIC MIGRATION...10

BUFFALO AND PRAIRIES...12

BUFFALO AND THE PLAINS INDIANS...14

THE BUFFALO DISAPPEARS...16

A PLACE FOR BUFFALO...18

LIFE IN A HERD...20

SPRING AND SUMMER...22

WINTER IN YELLOWSTONE...24

THREATS TO BUFFALO...26

SAVING THE BUFFALO...28

TYPES OF MIGRATION...30

GLOSSARY...31

FURTHER INFORMATION...32

INDEX...32

AMERICAN BUFFALO

Millions of American buffalo once grazed across much of North America. They roamed over the grassy **prairies**, mountains, and open forests. Huge herds moved together. The animals' snorting and grunting filled the air. When startled or in danger, the herds ran. They kicked up thick clouds of dust. They caused the ground to tremble. The herds never stayed in one place for long. They were always on the move, searching for fresh food to eat.

The buffalo's lifetime journey is their migration. This is when an animal moves from one **habitat** to another. Migrations happen for many reasons. Some animals move to be in warmer weather where there is more food. There they can reproduce, or have their babies. And these migrations can be long distances. Or they can be short distances, such as from a **plateau** to its valley. Sometimes migrations include both short and long distances, such as the buffalo's search for food.

Buffalo live in big groups called herds.

MIGRATION MAP

Wild buffalo live in small herds across the United States, Mexico, and Canada. The largest herd in the United States has more than 2,000 animals. This herd lives in Yellowstone National Park.

Yellowstone sits on a plateau, an area high above sea level. Yellowstone's buffalo migrate with the seasons. They have a **seasonal** migration. In summer, the buffalo graze over the high, grassy plateau. In fall, they migrate to the lower valleys. When winters are very cold, some buffalo migrate out of the park. In spring, they return to the plateau.

*This map shows the migration routes of buffalo
in Yellowstone National Park.*

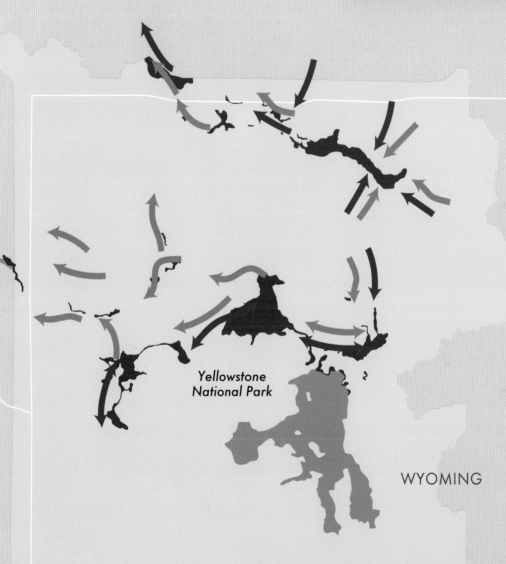

MONTANA

Buffalo Wintering Areas

Historic Buffalo Winter Movement

Recent Buffalo Winter Movement

Yellowstone
National Park

WYOMING

IDAHO

KINGS OF THE PRAIRIE

Buffalo are the largest land animals in North America. The males, or bulls, stand about 6 feet (2 m) high at the shoulder. They can weigh more than 2,000 pounds (1,000 kg). That's as much as four large grizzly bears! The females, or cows, are smaller. They weigh more than 1,000 pounds (454 kg), though.

Buffalo have huge humps at the shoulders. Buffalo have thick, heavy fur. It protects them from the cold in winter and hot sun in summer. They have large heads topped with mops of dark hair. Their heads are crowned with sharp, curved horns.

Scientists call buffalo "American bison." But when white settlers first came to North America, they called bison "buffalo." American bison are different animals than buffalo, which live in Asia and Africa. But the name stuck. Most people in the United States call these animals buffalo.

Buffalo are huge prairie animals.

LIKE THEIR CLOSE RELATIVES, COWS, BUFFALO CHEW THEIR FOOD AND SWALLOW IT. THE FOOD BREAKS DOWN INTO SMALLER PIECES IN THE STOMACH. THEN THE BUFFALO BRINGS THE FOOD BACK UP INTO THEIR MOUTHS AGAIN. THEY CHEW THE FOOD AGAIN AND SWALLOW IT. THIS HELPS BUFFALO EAT TOUGH, CHEWY GRASSES.

HISTORIC MIGRATION

American buffalo are grazers. They feed on grasses, **sedges**, and shrubs. Because they are large animals, they eat a lot of grass. They eat about 30 pounds (14 kg) a day. After they eat all the grass in one area, they move on to find more grass. To find enough food to eat, buffalo herds migrate.

Giant herds of buffalo once roamed North America. No one knows how many buffalo there were. Many think there were once 30 to 60 million. These herds migrated throughout the year. They went where food was growing in each season.

These giant herds no longer exist. No one knows what their migration routes looked like. A few of their routes remain as paths worn deep into the soil. They can still be seen from the air. Scientists have also learned about their migration by studying old buffalo bones. As a buffalo grazes, it gets minerals from its food. These minerals leave traces in the buffalo's bones. Scientists can study the traces to learn how and where buffalo once lived.

Buffalo graze on prairie grasses.

BUFFALO AND PRAIRIES

Many buffalo lived in the grasslands that once covered the middle of North America. These prairies went on in all directions. Prairies were the perfect place for animals that eat grass.

Many animals made prairies their home. **Predators** lived there, too. They included grizzly bears, wolves, and coyotes. But the buffalo was king. Vast herds of the large, shaggy animals once thundered across the prairie.

The prairie is an **ecosystem**. That is a place where all of the animals and plants live together. They depend on each other.

Many animals live in the prairies.

Buffalo help the prairie ecosystem in many ways. They dig up the soil with their sharp hooves. This pushes new seeds into the earth. It helps the prairie plants grow. Buffalo's grazing keeps the prairie grasses short. This makes the grasses grow even faster. The grazing also helps prairie dogs. They can watch for predators from the shorter grass.

Buffalo help other prairie animals, too. During the hot prairie summers, buffalo cool off by rolling on the ground. This makes dents in the ground called **wallows**. When rain comes, the wallows fill with water. The wallows turn into tiny ponds. Ducks and insects live in the ponds. Even the buffalo's droppings, called dung, are important. Buffalo dung puts **nutrients** in the soil. The rich soil is home to beetles and worms.

Wallows are made in the ground by buffalo.

HUNTING SUCH A LARGE, FAST ANIMAL WAS NOT EASY. NATIVE AMERICANS FOUND A WAY, THOUGH. THEY HUNTED BUFFALO BY DRIVING THE STAMPEDES OFF CLIFFS. LATER THEY HUNTED THEM FROM HORSEBACK USING GUNS OR BOWS AND ARROWS.

BUFFALO AND THE PLAINS INDIANS

For thousands of years, Native Americans lived in the prairies with the buffalo. The Plains Indians hunted buffalo and used every part of the animal. They ate buffalo meat. They used buffalo skin to make clothing and other things. They shaped the bones into tools. They used the rough tongue as a hairbrush. The dung was used as fuel for cooking.

The buffalo was important to the Plains Indians. They had deep respect for the animal. They honored the animals with songs and dances.

Native American tribes used buffalo hides, meat, and bones to make useful things.

THE BUFFALO DISAPPEARS

White settlers found millions and millions of buffalo when they moved to the prairies. But the settlers would almost cause the buffalo to disappear forever. The white settlers thought the buffalo were pests. They shot them in great numbers. Settlers thought they were unsafe for trains. When railroads were built across the prairies, buffalo stood on the tracks. Sometimes the animals pushed trains off the tracks. White hunters began shooting buffalo for their skins. The buffalo herds grew smaller and smaller.

In the late 1800s, few wild buffalo were left in the United States and Canada. People were afraid. They realized the buffalo could soon become **extinct**. This meant these animals could be lost forever.

Not only had the buffalo disappeared, but their prairie habitat had disappeared as well. Settlers had plowed the prairie. They destroyed the grasslands the buffalo needed. In the prairies, settlers grew fields of wheat, corn, and other crops.

Settlers moved to prairies and shot many buffalo.

A PLACE FOR BUFFALO

People thought Yellowstone National Park could be the one place where buffalo could live. The new park was the first national park in the world. It was created in 1872 to help protect wildlife in the United States. One of the last remaining buffalo herds was discovered hidden in a valley of the park. But it was very small. It only had about 20 animals.

People decided to act. Buffalo were brought from zoos and ranches to Yellowstone. The buffalo were released. Slowly the herd grew. Today the Yellowstone herd is a great success. It is one of the largest herds of wild buffalo in North America. In Yellowstone, the herd still migrates during the seasons.

Yellowstone National Park is home to the largest wild buffalo herd in North America.

LIFE IN A HERD

A buffalo herd is made of four to 20 adult females and their calves. The females stay together for life. The males stay with the herd until they are about three years old. Then they leave. Males live alone. Or they group together in small herds with other males.

Living in a herd helps the buffalo stay safe. In a herd they can group together. If a wolf or grizzly bear comes too close, the cows form a circle around the calves. If a bull is in the herd, the bull stands on the outside. The cows stand behind the bull. The adults lower their heads and point their large horns out. The calves stay safe inside the circle.

Running is another way buffalo stay safe. Buffalo can run fast—faster than most horses. Buffalo can reach up to 40 miles (65 km) an hour. They can also turn quickly when running. When a buffalo sees something unusual, it runs. Soon the whole herd runs and the ground shakes. This is called a stampede. The predator often cannot catch even one animal.

Herds include many females and their calves.

BUFFALO CAN HEAR VERY WELL. THEY CAN ALSO DETECT ODORS FROM MORE THAN 1 MILE (2 KM) AWAY.

SPRING AND SUMMER

Life for a Yellowstone buffalo begins in spring. That is the season when the mother buffalo give birth to their young. Each cow licks her orange–colored calf clean. Then the calf takes its first wobbly steps. Within a few hours it can walk.

In just a few weeks the calf stops drinking its mother's milk. Then it joins the rest of the herd to graze. With the herd always on the move, the calf must keep up. It is in danger if it wanders from the herd.

A calf's first spring and summer is a very important time. The calf must gain weight and grow strong to survive the winter. It needs to gain about six times its weight before the snow comes. By its first birthday, a buffalo may weigh more than 400 pounds (181 kg).

In summer, males and females come together to mate. Males battle to see which is stronger. They butt heads and push until one gives way. The winner gets to choose a mate.

A mother licks her newborn calf clean.

WINTER IN YELLOWSTONE

Buffalo are built to survive the cold. Their thick winter coats and layers of fat keep them warm. They might wander close to one of the hot springs in the park. The springs give the buffalo extra warmth. When the cold wind blows, they turn to face the wind. They shake the snow off their shaggy backs. To push aside snow, they lower their heads and sweep them from side to side.

Buffalo can even find food in winter. They press their noses into the snow and smell deeply. They can smell grass through 3 feet (1 m) of snow. When they find some, they dig with their sharp hooves. They reach the grass under the snow.

Buffalo know how to survive cold winters.

Winters can be very cold. Temperatures stay below freezing during the day. It gets even colder at night. Snowfall can be heavy. Some spots in the park get as much as 25 feet (8 m) of snow in a winter. That is enough to bury a two-story house.

In the winter, many of the buffalo leave the high plateau. They go to the warmer valleys. But sometimes, the snow becomes so deep that buffalo cannot dig to the grasses. They must leave to find food. Otherwise, they could starve.

The oldest female leads the herd along worn trails and river valleys. She makes a path through the deep snow. The herd follows in a straight line.

To stay alive, the calves must stay close to the herd. If a young buffalo wanders off the path, it could get stuck in deep snow. If it falls into an icy river, the buffalo might drown. Winter migration is a dangerous time for a young buffalo.

The herd walks through deep snow in search of food.

THREATS TO BUFFALO

Most winters, buffalo can find all the food they need inside Yellowstone. But sometimes the buffalo leave the park to find food. When Yellowstone's buffalo cross over the park's borders, they are in danger.

Inside Yellowstone, the buffalo are kept safe by law. People cannot hunt buffalo inside the park. But outside the park in Montana, buffalo can be shot and killed.

Why would someone shoot a buffalo? Some wild buffalo have a disease called **brucellosis**. This disease can also infect cattle. In pregnant cattle, the disease causes death of the calf. Ranchers fear the migrating buffalo will infect their cattle. They shoot and kill buffalo that wander too close to their ranches.

If buffalo wander outside of Yellowstone, they can be killed.

SAVING THE BUFFALO

Today the total number of buffalo in North America is about 200,000 to 250,000. Most live on ranches, where they are raised like cattle for meat. Ranch buffalo still look like their wild cousins, but they are different. Over time, ranchers have **domesticated** buffalo. They select only the most gentle animals to breed. Slowly the wildness in ranch buffalo has disappeared. Ranch buffalo do not fight or stampede. They spend all their lives on ranches. They also do not migrate.

Native American tribes are helping to restore wild buffalo. Today dozens of tribes have joined together to help. So far, the tribes have gathered herds that have almost 10,000 animals. Many tribes now have their own buffalo herds. And some still hunt the animals on horseback. They see the buffalo as an important part of Native American life.

Other wild herds, like the ones in Yellowstone, live on **reserves**. These reserves are found across the original land of buffalo. In these places, herds of wild buffalo still migrate like the buffalo that once filled the prairies.

Many buffalo now live on ranches and do not migrate.

TYPES OF MIGRATION

Different animals migrate for different reasons. Some move because of the climate. Some travel to find food or a mate. Here are the different types of animal migration:

Seasonal migration: This type of migration happens when the seasons change. Most animals migrate for this reason. Other types of migration, such as altitudinal and latitudinal, may also include seasonal migration.

Latitudinal migration: When animals travel north and south, it is called latitudinal migration. Doing so allows animals to change the climate where they live.

Altitudinal migration: This migration happens when animals move up and down mountains. In summer, animals can live higher on a mountain. During the cold winter, they move down to lower and warmer spots.

Reproductive migration: Sometimes animals move to have their babies. This migration may keep the babies safer when they are born. Or babies may need a certain habitat to live in after birth.

Nomadic migration: Animals may wander from place to place to find food in this type of migration.

Complete migration: This type of migration happens when animals are finished mating in an area. Then almost all of the animals leave the area. They may travel more than 15,000 miles (25,000 km) to spend winters in a warmer area.

Partial migration: When some, but not all, animals of one type move away from their mating area, it is partial migration. This is the most common type of migration.

Irruptive migration: This type of migration may happen one year, but not the next. It may include some or all of a type of animal. And the animal group may travel short or long distances.

> SOMETIMES ANIMALS NEVER COME BACK TO A PLACE WHERE THEY ONCE LIVED. THIS CAN HAPPEN WHEN HUMANS OR NATURE DESTROY THEIR HABITAT. FOOD, WATER, OR SHELTER MAY BECOME HARD TO FIND. OR A GROUP OF ANIMALS MAY BECOME TOO LARGE FOR AN AREA. THEN THEY MUST MOVE TO FIND FOOD.

GLOSSARY

brucellosis (broo-sell-LOW-sis): Brucellosis is a disease that harms cattle and buffalo. Buffalo can pass brucellosis to cattle.

domesticated (duh-MESS-tuh-kate-id): A domesticated animal is one that is not wild and can live with or by people. Many buffalo are now domesticated.

ecosystem (EE-koh-siss-tuhm): An ecosystem is a community of plants and animals that depend on each other and the land. A prairie is an ecosystem.

extinct (ek-STINGKT): A type of animal is extinct if it has died out. Buffalo almost became extinct.

habitat (HAB-uh-tat): A habitat is a place that has the food, water, and shelter an animal needs to survive. Buffalo move from one habitat to another.

nutrients (NOO-tree-untz): Nutrients are things that people, animals, and plants need to stay alive. Buffalo dung adds nutrients to the soil.

plateau (pla-TOH): A plateau is an area of high, flat land. In the winter, buffalo move from the plateau to the valleys.

prairies (PRAIR-eez): Prairies are large areas of grassy land with few or no trees. Prairies in the United States were once much bigger than they are today.

predators (PRED-uh-turs): Predators are animals that hunt and eat other animals. Predators live in the prairies.

reserves (ri-ZURVZ): Reserves are places that are set aside to keep animals and plants safe. Buffalo are safe on the reserves.

seasonal (SEE-zuhn-uhl): Seasonal is something related to the seasons of the year. A seasonal migration is when animals move from one place to another with the seasons.

sedges (SEJ-uhz): Sedges are plants that grow in wet ground. Buffalo eat sedges.

stampedes (stam-PEEDZ): Stampedes are when animals run wildly in one direction. Buffalo stampedes contain many animals.

wallows (WOL-ohz): Wallows are dents in the ground made by buffalo. Water collects in wallows made by buffalo.

FURTHER INFORMATION

Books

George, Jean Craighead. *The Buffalo Are Back.* New York: Dutton Children's Books, 2010.

Marrin, Albert. *Saving the Buffalo.* New York: Scholastic, 2006.

Patent, Dorothy Hinshaw, and William Munoz. *The Buffalo and the Indians: A Shared Destiny.* New York: Clarion, 2006.

Waldman, Neil. *They Came from the Bronx: How the Buffalo Were Saved from Extinction.* Honesdale, PA: Boyds Mills Press, 2001.

Web Sites

Visit our Web site for links about buffalo migration: *childsworld.com/links*

Note to Parents, Teachers, and Librarians:

We routinely verify our Web links to make sure they are safe and active sites. So encourage your readers to check them out!

INDEX

bison, 9
bodies, 9
brucellosis, 26
calves, 20, 22, 23, 25, 26
Canada, 6, 17
defenses, 4, 20, 21
dung, 13, 15
eating, 4, 10, 11, 24, 25, 26

herds, 4, 6, 11, 12, 16, 19, 20, 22, 25, 29
hunting, 14, 15, 16, 26, 29
mating, 23
Mexico, 6
migration route, 6
Plains Indians, 15
plateau, 5, 6, 25

prairies, 4, 9, 12, 13, 15, 16, 17, 29
predators, 12, 13, 20
ranches, 19, 26, 29
reserves, 29
settlers, 9, 16, 17
stampedes, 14, 20, 29
United States, 6, 9, 17
wallows, 13

winters, 6, 9, 23, 24, 25, 26
Yellowstone National Park, 6, 19, 22, 26, 29